SAN DIEGO WHERE CALIFORNIA BEGAN

Fifth Edition, Revised

by
James R. Mills

SAN DIEGO
HISTORICAL SOCIETY
1985

Contents

COVER: "Mission San Diego de Alcala," by
Edith Buckland Webb

ENDPAPERS: Front, Dan O'Leary, c. 1900; and
the schooner "Irene," c. 1903. Back, San Diego
store fronts along the west side of Sixth
Avenue in 1887.

TITLE PAGE: Bells at the Adobe Chapel
in Old Town, 1898

PRECEEDING PAGES: Ruins of Mission San Diego,
c. 1880s; and City Guard Band in front of
the Horton House, 1890.

OPPOSITE: Birdseye View of San Diego, 1883

Unless otherwise noted all photographs used
in this booklet are from the San Diego Historical
Society's Title Insurance and Trust Collection

San Diego's native population tended towards vegetarianism. Here, in a photograph taken in the early part of this century, a native woman demonstrates grinding with milling stones.

"In the beginning the Indians of this port showed themselves very haughty and arrogant . . . They are very intelligent Indians, noisy, bold, great traders, covetous, and thievish." In these terms did Father Francisco Palou introduce San Diego's native people to the Spanish world in his *Historical Memoirs of New California,* written soon after the founding of San Diego. He wrote further, "All the men go naked and most of them are painted, but the women are covered modestly in front with woven fibers and behind with the skins of animals. They go armed with bows and quivers of arrows."

The native population who lived near what is presently the modern city of San Diego were called Diegueños by the Spanish. Anthropologists now call the Diegueño people north of the San Diego River the Ipai and the more southeastern people the Tipai. Linguistically, these natives were related to the Yuma people. They tended toward vegetarianism, acorns were an especially important part of their diet, and tribes fought battles for the possession of oak groves. The mortars, *manos* or milling stones and stone pestles now found all over the county were used to grind acorns into flour, which was boiled into gruel in pottery bowls. Diegueños also ate various kinds of seeds. They did not scorn meat, but they were basically foragers. They killed rabbits, crows, mice, snakes, frogs, coyotes, and crawfish with weapons that varied from arrows and slings, to clubs, throwing sticks, and bare hands. Ocean and bay beaches provided shellfish, a staple of their diet. Fishing was done by means of weir, net and, less often, from canoes with hook and line. From the seashore to the valleys, the mountain oak groves and on to the desert, they roamed in search of food.

There were a few creatures they did not eat, for religious reasons. Sacred and not to be considered as food were squirrels, bears, doves, pigeons, and mudhens.

Along the coast, families were likely to occupy basket-like huts of tules; inland, the huts would be of brush or branches. Dwellings of blood-clan groups were gathered together in villages of as many as three hundred people. Valleys, such as that of the San Diego River, were heavily populated because of their trees and water, and of the animals which these things attracted. Knowing no metals, they might be called a Stone Age people; their tools were fashioned from stone, wood, bone and shell. Soapstone from the Channel Islands occasionally was used for vessels. Sandstone was fashioned everywhere. It even was used for *metates* and grinding bowls along the coast, although for this a harder rock was preferred. Pottery, an exception throughout most of California, was common for the storage of water and food.

In 1602 Sebastián Vizcaíno noted that

9

Natives near the coast were likely to occupy basket-like huts of tules; inland the huts would be of brush or branches.

the men went "naked and besmeared with black and white paint ... wearing many feathers." The paint was used to frighten away both mortal enemies and evil spirits. Random tattooing was common, and more popular among the women than the men. Two or three vertical lines on a feminine chin were thought beautifying; they were commonly worked into the skin, as a part of adolescence ceremonies, by an artist using cactus spines to prick charcoal through the surface.

Because there was little tribal organization, crimes usually went unpunished, although sometimes damages were demanded by an aggrieved survivor of a murder victim. When an execution was conducted, arrows were the instruments employed. At such times the action was one of vengeance, effected by relatives of the dead man; retribution by a group or society was unknown.

Rock art painting among the Diegueño was highly developed. It was abstract and geometric entirely. Diegueños also practiced sand painting, carved bone and ceramic etching. Creation myths were varied, as were other legends. Animate and inanimate objects were personified; the bear, like the eagle, was venerated, and the porpoise was thought by the coastal people to be the guardian of the world. Medicine-men were much respected. They treated localized ills by sucking the blood from the painful area, by blowing smoke on it, or by spitting on it. Some of the medicine-men specialized, setting themselves up as snake-bite experts, headache men, rainmakers and so forth. The headache specialists often pretended to suck the demons, which were responsible for the misery, out of the victim's skull; the demons actually were animals or reptiles small enough to be concealed in the specialist's mouth.

The local natives failed to arouse great enthusiasm among some Europeans. Baron von Humboldt gave them a low classification, along with the Tasmanians, but admitted that in large numbers, they could be dangerous. In 1787 Pedro Fages, Spanish governor of California, described them as "... absolutely opposed to all rational subjection and full of the spirit of independence" and bluntly added that "... a considerable armed force must be on hand ... to repress their natural and crusty pride." From a non-European view, however, these traits can be considered positive. The Diegueño resisted the Spaniards and hoped for trade through reciprocity. Better organized natives might have overpowered the Spanish powers sent to California and delayed settlement indefinitely, perhaps long enough for some other European power to occupy the land and so change the course of history.

10

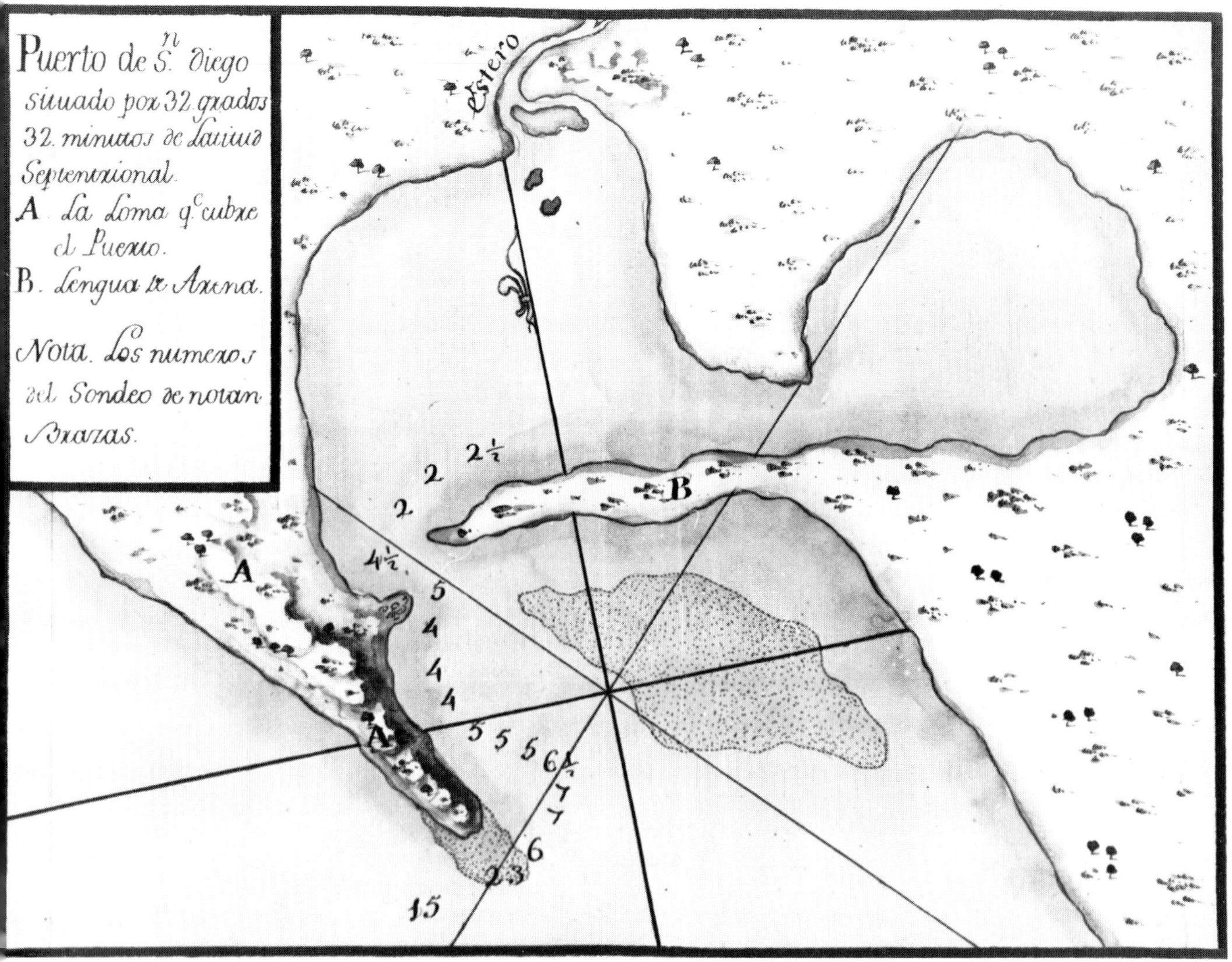

Puerto de S.ⁿ Diego
situado por 32 grados
32. minutos de Latitud
Septentrional.
A. La Loma q.^e cubre
el Puerto.
B. Lengua de Arena.

Nota. Los numeros
del Sondeo denotan
Brazas.

Estero

A
A

B

$2\frac{1}{2}$
2 2
2
$4\frac{1}{2}$
5
4
4
4
5 5
5 6
6
7
6
2 3
15

Archivo Historico Nacional, Madrid

Part 2 Spanish Rule

Point Loma was the first rugged foreland of golden California to rise above the horizon to European eyes. Spanish explorers called it *The Point of California.* Its name has changed since, like that of the admiral who discovered it. Born in Portugal, he was baptized João Rodrígues, although among Spaniards he was known as Juan Rodríguez. Another name, Cabrilho, followed his surname; it apparently referred to the village of his birth. Later Californians changed it to Cabrillo, a Spanish form of the word. He qualified himself for leadership while serving the king of Spain as a soldier under Cortés, during wars in Mexico and Central America.

In June of 1542 he sailed northward from Navidad, on the west coast of Mexico, to explore the northwest coast of the continent to find out what was on it and how far it extended. Most important, he was to search for the mythical Straits of Anian—known to the English as the Northwest Passage—supposed to extend from the Atlantic to the Pacific through, or above North America, providing a convenient route for voyagers to Cathay, the Spice Islands, and the Spanish colonies on the Pacific Coast. If France, England, or another enemy discovered the Straits first, Spain's future would be gravely affected.

Cabrillo was given two little vessels, only partly decked over, to carry his expedition on a hard voyage up a wild, unexplored coast, against the prevailing winds. The ships were named *San Salvador* and *Victoria.* They were among a number built by Cabrillo himself, with the aid of Spanish overseers and Indian workmen. They were of native materials, except that the iron-work and finished articles were brought from Spain to Mexico and transported across the continent from Gulf ports.

The ships were far from well found for a long voyage to windward, being open, stubby, and small, yet Cabrillo reached San Diego 103 days out, on September 28, discovering the point, the bay, and Upper California itself. He called the harbor "San Miguel." In his official diary he said, "Being in this port there passed a very great tempest, but on account of this port's being very good they suffered nothing."

The Spaniards remained here six days, then sailed northward. While landing at San Miguel Island at the western end of Santa Barbara Channel, Cabrillo broke his leg (or arm, the two accounts of the voyage differ) but he did not delay there. Off the coast of Northern California, November storms drove him back. He returned to San Miguel Island to weather the gales and recuperate. He died there of his broken limb, an earlier victim than Hudson or Franklin of the search for the Straits of Anian. Cabrillo's pilot, Ferrelo, pushed northward again perhaps as far as Cape

Mendocino, and did not get back to New Spain until April of 1543.

During the latter part of the sixteenth century Sir Francis Drake, Sir Thomas Cavendish, and other freebooters came into the Pacific Ocean, raiding and plundering, and Drake claimed Northern California for England in 1579. The Spanish government's interest in the Straits of Anian became more vital. Also an urgent need arose for a haven for the Manila galleons during their run with the westerly winds of the North Pacific to Acapulco. Refuge from northern storms was no less important than a place of safety from buccaneers. The Manila trade would make the merchants involved fabulously rich if even half of the ships were lost, but how much better it would be if more could be brought through!

By 1602 the galleons had been running regularly for almost forty years. They were to keep up a scheduled service for over two centuries more, until 1815, and become the longest lived line in maritime history.

San Diego Gets Its Name

On May 5 of 1602 Sebastián Vizcaíno, who had been on the great galleon *Santa Ana* when it was captured by Cavendish off lower California, was sent with three good ships, the *San Diego*, which he made his flagship, the *Santo Tomás,* and the launch *Tres Reyes,* to explore the coast of Califor-

nia. On November 10 Vizcaíno anchored under the lee of Point Loma, five months out from Acapulco.

Two days later—on the feast day of San Diego de Alcalá, a Spanish Franciscan who lived in the fifteenth century—priests with the expedition set up a chapel on Ballast Point and there held the first Catholic service conducted on Californian soil. On that day the bay was renamed for San Diego—in honor of the day and the flagship. Declaring that Cabrillo's recorded observations were too inaccurate to identify positively the points he had visited, Vizcaíno changed the rest of the names set down by his predecessor.

The Spaniards stayed ten days while their ships were scraped and repaired. Vizcaíno described San Diego in his journal as, ". . . a port which must be the best to be found in all the South Sea (the Pacific) . . . protected on all sides and having a good anchorage." Although Vizcaíno recommended this as an ideal port for the Manila fleet, when he saw Monterey Bay he said that haven was even better, partly because of the forests of tall trees which could be worked into spars and masts, to repair damage from weather or gunfire.

He returned to Mexico after a difficult struggle northward to find the Straits. Forty of his men died of scurvy during the voyage. The admiral once wrote in his journal, "The sick were dying of hunger

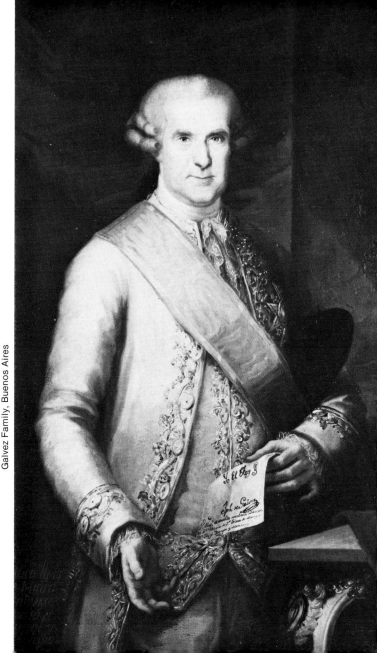

José de Galvéz, Inspector General of Mexico.

because they could not eat what was on board the ship on account of their sore mouths."

To the government of New Spain Vizcaíno recommended that settlements could and should be established in California. He organized an expedition, under the authority of the Viceroy, to capitalize upon his voyage of exploration, but his destination was ordered changed to Rico de Oro and Rico de Plata, mythical islands, of which the Spanish had heard rumors.

California was forgotten. One hundred and sixty-seven years passed before white men again entered San Diego Bay. Occasionally Point Loma was sighted by the castled galleons heaving along under slowly lifting, white-bellied sails, on the long searoad from Manila to Mexico.

Foreign Threats

Not until Spain's absentee ownership of California, established by right of discovery, was challenged, did settlement ensue. In the late eighteenth century the Russians, who had advanced rapidly across Siberia and the North Pacific into Alaska, began to move southward. Fear that they might occupy the harbors of California, and become a threat to the Spanish hold on Mexico and its riches, caused King Charles to direct that steps be taken to establish royal control of the land.

In 1768 the Inspector General of Mexico,

José de Galvéz, undertook to organize five expeditions at La Paz, Lower California, three to come by sea and two by land, to settle California. On January 9, 1769, the first contingent set sail in the supply ship *San Carlos;* on February 15 more followed in the ship *San Antonio,* and, a little later, the last to set out from the harbor of La Paz left in another vessel, the *San Jose.*

On April 29 the *San Antonio* sailed into San Diego Bay, the first ship since Vizcaíno's. The *San Carlos,* which departed over a month before the *San Antonio,* was nowhere to be seen. For two anxious weeks the *San Antonio* swung to her anchors just inside Ballast Point, quite alone. Then the *San Carlos* came in, after having sailed too far north—in accordance with Cabrillo's directions; Vizcaíno's had been ignored. Two dozen of the 62-man crew of the ship were dead of scurvy; only four sailors could stand up and help work the ship, and it was beyond their power to lower a boat when they arrived. The crew of the *San Antonio* had to take them off. A rude, canvas hospital was set up on the beach for the sick men. The men of both ships settled down to await the *San José* which never did come in, and never was heard of again.

On May 14, Captain Fernando Rivera y Moncadá led the advance party of the overland expedition to the shores of the bay. With him came seventy men, including Father Juan Crespí, who kept an account

Father Junípero Serra founded the first mission in upper California in 1769.

of the journey. Finding the ships' complements camped by the bay in terrible physical condition, Rivera moved the bivouac to the Old Town area, and set up hospital, corral, and brush hut headquarters for all, thereby choosing the site of San Diego. In time, fresh food and livestock he brought improved the health of the men. Supplies for the expeditions were largely provided by the missions of Lower California, which had been taken from the Jesuits in 1767 and given to the Franciscans temporarily to serve as bases for expansion into Upper California.

The Coming of Serra

Gaspár de Portolá, the first governor of California and commander of the entire colonization effort, which was called "The Sacred Expedition of 1769," rode in on June 27, and two days later the rest of his party arrived with Junípero Serra, the new Father President of the yet-unfounded mission chain. In a few days Portolá set out again to the northward to search for the wonderful bay of Monterey, described by Sebastián Vizcaíno as an excellent place to make the center of California development.

San Diego was officially founded July 16 on a hill above Rivera's camp, a hill chosen for its commanding view of Mission Valley with its large native population, of the bay, and the area surrounding. Father Serra, after a solemn mass, dedicated the first mission in California to the glory of God. In the same ceremony he dedicated the first presidio—or military settlement—whose walls were to surround and protect the mission. Both were named San Diego, in honor of the saint for whom Vizcaino had named the port. Earthworks for defense and huts for shelter were soon thrown up to create the first foothold of European civilization in California on Presidio Hill, which has become known, consequently, as "The Plymouth Rock of the Pacific Coast."

The presidio took the form of a square, about the size of a modern city block, within ramparts that developed from earthworks and palisades into adobe walls with bastions mounting brass cannon. Buildings housing officers, troops, supplies, and the mission formed a smaller rectangle surrounding an open parade ground and the commandant's house. In the middle of the south wall stood the great gate, the only way in. Through it came the Franciscan fathers, from other missions in Upper and Lower California, and the soldiers of the king, with their lances, shields, flintlocks, and banners.

The danger from the native population was considered so great that neither private citizen nor missionary was allowed to leave the protection of the walls without a military escort. The mission failed to grow because of the lack of tillable land near the presidio and because the natives feared and distrusted the soldiers. In 1774 permission was received to remove San Diego Mission to its present site about five miles up the valley, where there was a large native village called *Nipaguay*. Ground was broken during the fall of 1774, but on November 4, four hundred natives from the El Capitan area, taking advantage of the mission's exposure, attacked and burned the building.

California's first Christian martyr was Father Luis Jayme, who, after the attack commenced, walked out the door with his arms outstretched, saying, "Love God, my children." His lifeless body was found the next day. Father Serra, on receiving word of the martyrdom, said, "Thanks be to God! That land is already irrigated; now the conversion of the Diegueños will succeed."

Some of the natives who carried out the assault returned to become mission neophytes. Mission San Diego, rededicated in 1777, soon boasted flourishing vineyards, and orchards of olives, dates, and pears. Herds of cattle, horses, and sheep spread over the rolling hills.

Mission Days

The mission, like the presidio, was built in the form of a square, but it enclosed beautiful gardens, irrigated by water brought from a dam miles up the river, via California's first aqueduct.

Natives worked in the gardens, orchards,

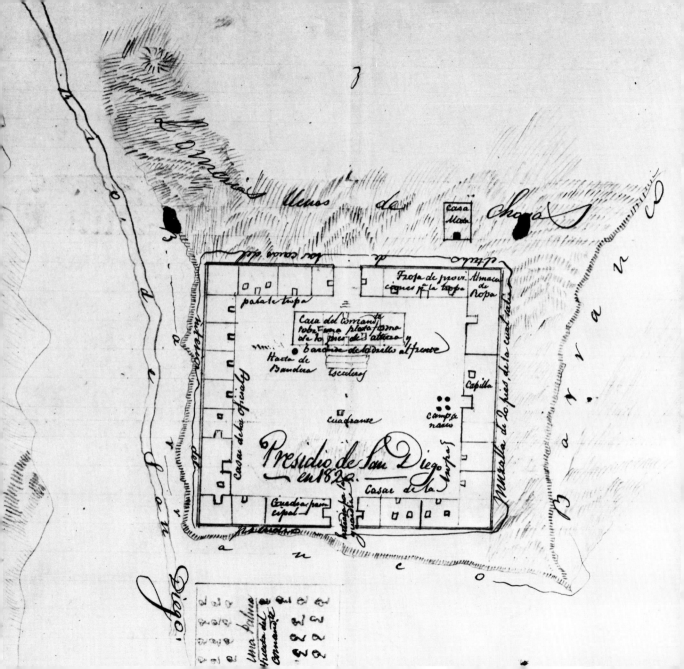

Presidio de San Diego en 1820.

fields, and ranges. Their day began with a morning mass; a breakfast of *pozole* or ground barley boiled with meat, vegetables, or, on special occasions, chocolate. Beans and beef were staples for the evening meal after the angelus.

The system was patriarchal. Unmarried neophytes were locked in barracks at night to put them beyond temptation to sin. Married couples lived in villages of huts outside. Corporal punishment was inflicted upon those who broke the rules laid down for them; floggings and confinements in the stocks were employed.

Life was leisurely and undisturbed by the rest of the world, until 1793, when the English explorer, George Vancouver came. He and the Spaniards enjoyed very cordial relations, but he publicized the excellence of the harbor in his reports and remarked on its need for protection from attack. He recommended Ballast Point as the best location for a harbor defense fortification. The Spanish followed his suggestion to the letter, and built Fort Guijarros, named for the point, which they called Point Guijarros—"Point Cobblestones"—because of its shingle beach.

The first American ship to enter the harbor was the little brig *Betsy,* which came in on August 25, 1800, for wood and water. Word of the abundance of sea otters brought more Yankees, for the otters' skins commanded high prices in China. In 1803 the ship *Alexander* tried to smuggle five hundred of them out of San Diego, but was prevented by the authorities. Later in the year the brig *Lelia Byrd* was arrested for the same reason. A duel between the guns of the ship and fort, after the *Lelia Byrd's* crew overpowered the guards set over them and put out to sea, has been dignified with the name The Battle of San Diego. The fort's gunners were driven to cover in this, the only time San Diego's harbor defense guns were fired in action.

Time passed uneventfully until 1812, when a great earthquake shook down the mission church. The 1813 reconstruction gave the mission much of its present form and appearance. Converts increased in numbers and, in 1818, the asistencia, or mission outpost, was established at Santa Ysabel with a small chapel.

Hippolyte de Bouchard, the Argentine pirate who sacked Monterey and Capistrano, aroused a great deal of excitement here in 1818, although he failed to show up. The presidio garrison could have done nothing if he had come. They were few and ill-equipped. The military establishment was a poor orphan, administratively, being so far from army sources of supply and finance. The missions had to feed and clothe the troops, although to a large extent the soldiers were left to shift for themselves.

Yet they remained loyal to the Spanish

crown during the revolutionary wars, as did the Franciscans, whose hold on their lands depended on royal support and power. In 1821, however, one of the king's most important officers in Mexico, General Agustín de Iturbide, swung his army over to the side of independence and declared himself Emperor Agustín I of Mexico.

Although the event seemed far away, it ushered California into a new era. No longer a province in the realm of the Spanish Bourbons, it had become a Mexican dependency. The mission period would close as a result, and that of the ranchos would begin.

A water color drawing of the San Diego Hide Houses at La Playa made by a sailor on the USS Cyane.

Part 3 Mexican Interlude

Californians heard of the successful revolution in Mexico when the battles were long past. The news meant little, for the influence of the national government seemed unimportant in their lives. On April 20, 1822, the Mexican flag was raised over the presidio and San Diegans swore their allegiance to it. Luis Argüello was appointed the first Mexican governor.

In 1825 the presidio became, at least informally, the capital of both Upper and Lower California, much to the disgust of the residents of the usual capital, Monterey. The change was due to a preference for San Diego on the part of the new governor, José María Echeandía. A tall, dignified Spaniard who suffered from rheumatism, he was fond of San Diego's equable climate. He also was fond, it is said, of a beautiful San Diego girl named Josefa Carrillo. Although the fondness was all on his side, he did not wish to leave a town which was graced by the presence of the lovely Josefa.

During the 1820s what is now called Old Town came into existence. The Christianization of the natives and the lessening of fear of attacks by foreign enemies, together with the disappearance of royal control over the presidio, encouraged people with orchards and gardens outside the walls to build houses convenient to their plots of land. Captain Francisco María Ruíz, the commander of the presidio, was the first to build at the bottom of the hill. By 1829 San Diego was described as being a collection of thirty rude houses, mostly occupied by retired soldiers and their extensive families. The presidio, with its dwindling garrison, began to decay.

The town in general, however, was prospering at that time. Annual port revenues rose to $34,000, six times those of San Francisco, as a result of the development of the hide trade. There were few people in California and no intensive agriculture, but the hills abounded with the descendants of the cattle the Franciscan missionaries had brought when they came to establish the mission chain. The animals' hides came to be called "California banknotes" and were the one thing of real value for export that the economy produced. The hide trade opened in 1822 with the arrival on the bay's placid waters of the ship *Sachem*, of Boston.

Traffic in Hides

When Yankee entrepreneurs learned of the abundance of cheap hides in California, they dispatched ships by the dozen. From Californians of good families and backgrounds requests for grants of land poured into the state capital—wherever it happened to be at the time—for the governor's action. The various governors granted range land by the square league, with the cattle on it, virtually for the asking. The

25

herds were improvidently slaughtered for their hides and tallow; little of even the best meat was butchered out of the carcass. Buzzards and coyotes grew fat and multitudinous.

San Diego became the depot for the trade. Ships of many flags gathered hides along the coast and brought them to San Diego to be cured. Hide houses, barnlike in size and appearance, were erected along the beach inside Ballast Point. Each bore the name of the ship for which it served as a base.

An international settlement grew up, of crewmen who cleaned the fresh hides and cured them in brine. Dana's immortal description of this community, facetiously called "Hide Park," in his book *Two Years Before the Mast,* makes a fascinating picture.

To trade for the hides the Boston ships brought guns, powder, hardware, toilet articles, woolens, cotton goods, boots, shoes and other items from the Atlantic states. China was the source of silk sashes, shawls and rebozos. Perfumes and liquors came from France. All were displayed below decks aboard the ships, in sales rooms created by the fixing in place of temporary bulkheads.

The day that a ship's snowy canvas began to lift above the horizon beyond Point Loma was a day of anticipation for the womenfolk of San Diego's "California-bank-note-wealthy" ranch owners. It was a great social event to be taken out by the ship's boats, along with all the other ladies in town, to look over stocks that one had never seen before.

The ladies were extravagant spenders. They wanted only the best, and a great deal of that. They were no less lavish with their time, covering with embroidery everything they bought, from clothes to curtains and bedclothes.

People lived chiefly upon beef, corn, and beans, often in combinations such as tamales and chili con carne. They entertained themselves with celebrations of religious fiestas, with rodeos to demonstrate their prowess as vaqueros, with bull fights (in which anyone could participate), with bull and bear fights, and with revolutionary activities. The people took part as principals in all these diversions.

Yankee Jitters

Yankee visitors from the sea were accepted into citizenship, church, and family by Mexican Californians, but fear of expansion to the coast by the United States remained constantly with the officials, who lived in apprehension of overland invasion. It was felt that Americans could be kept in hand so long as they came by sea as merchants, in controllable numbers. However, any overland communication might fill the vacant land of California with acquisitive foreigners.

The first American to come across the deserts into California arrived in San Diego January 1, 1827, to start the year wrong for the governor. He was the famous trapper and trail blazer Jedediah Smith, known as "The Bible Toter" because he never went anywhere without a copy of the good book. This man had discovered the trails which became the highways of the westward movement, the Oregon Trail, the California Trail, and lesser routes all through the great West.

Governor Echeandía had him thrown in jail. Only the intercession of the Americans belonging to the ships on the bay effected his release; he was sent on his way after he had promised never to return to California. But now the way was broken across the wastes and the tide was bound to follow it.

In 1828 Sylvester Pattie of Kentucky came into town from the east via Lower California, with eight trappers. Among them was his son James Ohio Pattie. The entire party was jailed in a bastion of the presidio wall, and the elder Pattie died while in prison. James spent his days plotting revenge against the Governor, whom he held responsible. Echeandía made attempts to show kindness to the angry young man, but found his overtures rebuffed. James gained his freedom in return for agreeing to vaccinate all the people, white and red, in California, with a small phial of vaccine he had brought with him on his journeys. It appears that the governor, far from having believed that so little vaccine could do so great a work, simply wanted to be gracefully rid of the young fire eater.

Los Insurrectos

Echeandía's partiality to San Diego, together with the general destitution of the too-often unpaid soldiers, promoted revolution in the north in 1829. The presidio of San Diego then bustled with activity. The blacksmith toiled long hours repairing guns, sharpening swords, and manufacturing the favorite weapon of Californians, the makeshift lance. The governor marched away with the men of San Diego, who bore the tools of war the smith had forged. At Santa Barbara and Monterey they contacted the northerners and found that the insurrection faded away in the face of authority. This uprising, called the Solis Insurrection after its leader Joaquin Solis, was the first of a series of rebellions that lasted until the Mexican flag was hauled down in the plazas and the Stars and Stripes replaced it.

In 1830 Manuel Victoria was sent from Mexico to be the new governor, and moved the capital to Monterey. He proved to be an autocrat, banishing people from their California homes for real or fanciful reasons. Some of the exiles, including the powerful landowners Abel Stearns and

Abel Stearns, a large Californian landowner.

José Carrillo, got only as far as San Diego on their involuntary journeys to the border. While here they discussed the situation with Juan Bandini and Pío Pico. Conversation ripened into conspiracy. The participants walked up the hill to the presidio, and as no attack was anticipated, captured the post easily and took control of the town. They then persuaded Echeandía to join them and lead the revolt, and off they went northward, taking Los Angeles on the way, and meeting Victoria at Cahuenga Pass (now on the 101 freeway between Hollywood and North Hollywood). The forces joined battle, more or less, and two men were killed. Echeandía's men ran away and Victoria retired to San Gabriel Mission, where he resigned his position, leaving the post of governor to Echeandía, who soon had revolutions of his own to deal with.

Confusion reigned until 1833, when José Figueroa, a brevet brigadier general and former governor of Sinaloa and Sonora, arrived from Mexico with a federal appointment as governor. An administrator made extremely able by experience and temperament, he is remembered as the best Mexican governor of California. However, his many merits are somewhat offset by his being the executive who implemented government orders to secularize church property. He granted mission lands to private individuals, thereby stripping thousands of natives of the protection of the Church at a time when they were not equipped by aptitude or training to compete with white men on the latters' terms. Santiago Argüello (a brother of the ex-governor) received the ranges of the San Diego Mission from a later governor, as Figueroa's policy was carried out by his successors.

A Town Is Born

In 1834 San Diego became a *pueblo*—or town— officially, instead of a military post, and civil rule had its beginnings. Juan Maria Osuna was elected first *alcalde,* or mayor, although his functions included some judicial ones not usually associated with that office. By 1838, however, the population of San Diego had decreased so much that the settlement was deprived of the dignity of the title *pueblo* and simply made a department of the pueblo of Los Angeles. By 1840 only 140 persons called San Diego home. The presidio was crumbling away. There is a story that the garrison finally was reduced to one man and then disbanded, if the act could be called that, for lack of funds. At last the tiles and furnishings of the old fort were sold by an officer to defray the back pay that the government owed him. This left the adobe walls unprotected; the rain soon reduced them to the hillocks of mud which are all that are left of the first settlement on the Pacific Coast of the United States, and the one-time capital of Upper and Lower California. In 1840 the contents of Fort Guijarros were sold to Juan Machado for $40. San Diego ceased to be a military town.

The decline had been steady, although far from peaceful. In 1836 Juan B. Alvarado had attained the governorship of California through a revolution that he led to achieve that end. He favored centering governmental activities in Monterey. Southern Californians protested in vain. At last Juan Bandini and Santiago Arguello organized a revolution and seized Los Angeles, in order to overthrow the power of Governor Alvarado in the South. Native troubles in San Diego required the attention of the revolutionaries, so they left Los Angeles to return to San Diego and deal with the problems arising at home.

Bandini's Army

Once San Diego's natives were pacified, Bandini enlisted the white men of the town into what he called the Army of the Supreme Government. About one hundred strong it marched north to attack Alvarado's authority. At San Luis Rey the force was overtaken by a Mexican commissioner, who had been sent to California by the federal government to put a new national constitution into effect here. The revolutionary army happily took the oath of allegiance to the new government, and continued northward with the commissioner to help effect the changes required by the

Republic of Mexico and thereby overthrow the state government. At Los Angeles the citizens staged a fiesta to welcome the arrivals and the change, and everyone took the new oath of allegiance.

Governor Alvarado raised an army and led it south to suppress the insurrection. At Santa Barbara he encountered the federal commissioner, who was on his way north. Alvarado volunteered to take the oath, too, and was confirmed by the commissioner as governor. The Army of the Supreme Government, cheated out of a good revolution, disconsolately turned its face toward San Diego once more.

In October 1837 Carlos Antonio Carrillo of San Diego claimed to have received an appointment from Mexico as governor. He was accepted by Southern California but Alvarado refused to relinquish control in the North. Carrillo strengthened his hold on San Diego by declaring Monterey and San Francisco closed as ports of entry, and by establishing a custom house here. Alvarado sent an army south to relieve Santa Barbara which, because of its loyalty to him, was being beseiged by Carrillo forces. Alvarado also instructed his men to take Los Angeles and hold it. After a few skirmishes the northerners accomplished their missions.

Carrillo retreated to San Diego to raise a new army with the help of Juan Bandini and others. With about a hundred men supported by three cannon, Carrillo moved northward toward Los Angeles. At Las Flores, just north of the site of Oceanside, he met Alvarado. After an indecisive battle that amounted to very little in the way of violence, the two governors of California met in a conference in which Alvarado outmaneuvered Carrillo and kept not only the office of governor but also Carrillo's three cannon.

Five Hundred Jailbirds

In 1842 Alvarado was finally replaced by a new governor who could enforce his claims. This man was Manuel Micheltorena, who was sent from Mexico to strengthen the nation's hold on its turbulent northwestern province in the face of growing American population and interest in the area. Yankees were crossing the mountains to settle around Sutter's Fort and Sonoma. The Mexican government feared another revolution like that in Texas, and was concerned about what to do with an increasingly expensive accumulation of prisoners in Mexican jails. Therefore the new governor was given the support of five hundred convicts who accepted a pardon proffered to those who would enlist in the army. A miserable lot, these troops were called "Micheltorena's cholos" by native Californios.

Alfred Robinson described the unhappy soldiers in his book *Life in California*

Pio Pico, the last Mexican governor of California.

before the Conquest in these words: "Not one individual among them possessed a jacket or pantaloons, but naked and like the savages, they concealed their nudity with dirty, miserable blankets."

Quiet San Diego was changed by their coming. Robinson wrote: "Day after day the place resounded with the noise of the trumpet and the drums; and a level spot, on the river's margin, was the scene of military maneuvers. At night the gardens and vineyards were plundered, and neighboring farms suffered greatly, from the frequency of the soldiers' visits." Women could not leave washed clothes unwatched to dry, nor suppers boiling in the kitchen, but some miscreant would steal them. Nothing was safe that had value.

Micheltorena favored Monterey as the capital of the province, despite the fact that the south insisted that Los Angeles should be the seat of government. His departure with his soldiers, for Monterey, did not arouse universal displeasure in San Diego.

Pio Pico and Juan Alvarado raised the banner of rebellion in 1844, and San Diegans flocked to their colors. Los Angeles became the point of concentration and center of activities. The men of the revolution joined battle with Micheltorena's soldiers at Cahuenga Pass, as the governor approached Los Angeles to put down the uprising. After two horses and one mule

The USS Cyane brought John Fremont to San Diego in 1846.

were killed in an artillery duel which took no human lives, Micheltorena capitulated, and agreed to leave California and take his *cholos* with him. Pico assumed power and made Los Angeles his capital. Californian dependence on Mexico ended then to all intents and purposes.

"Operation Premature"

The flow of American frontiersmen had been continuing into Northern California. Under the mistaken belief that war with Mexico had been declared, the United States Navy had attacked and seized Monterey—then the capital—during Micheltorena's time. The Pacific squadron of frigates was obviously ready to repeat the conquest when the inevitable war over disputed boundaries did break out in reality.

Sure that war would result in American acquisition of his province, Governor Pico, wishing to provide for friends, relatives, and other longtime residents of California, granted away thousands of square miles of land during the last year before hostilities commenced. Among the grants was the largest of all the ranchos in San Diego County, Santa Margarita (now Camp Pendleton), comprising 133,400 acres. He presented it to himself and his brother Andrés.

In 1846 American troops under Major John C. Fremont, who had been sent out to California to survey and warned not to fight, assisted Americans from Sonoma to Fort Sutter in the establishment of the temporarily independent Bear Flag Republic. The Navy took Monterey, as expected, and the long-threatened war came to California.

On July 29 the United States Sloop-of-War *Cyane*, commanded by Captain Samuel Dupont, stood into the port of San Diego bringing John Fremont and the battalion of California volunteers from the Bear Flag country. With them was Kit Carson, the scout.

Captain Dupont sent Lieutenant Stephen C. Rowan, U.S.N., ashore with a boatload of sailors and marines to raise the flag in the Plaza. There was no opposition.

34

Ten days after the Stars and Stripes fluttered up the pole in the Plaza, Fremont rode north at the head of his battalion, on a beautiful sorrel horse given to him by Juan Bandini. His volunteers advanced against Los Angeles, to rendezvous with Navy units which had debarked at San Pedro; in short order Los Angeles was in American hands, although only temporarily.

San Diego, left almost unprotected, invited attack by Californians loyal to Mexico, who began to concentrate within striking distance. The few Americans holding the town fled to the safety of the Yankee whaler *Stonington,* lying in the bay, and again the Mexican flag floated over the town.

The refugees on the whale ship were disturbed by the existence of two ancient Spanish cannon on Presidio Hill. The possibility that the Mexicans might bring them down to the water's edge to bombard the *Stonington* drove the Americans to take preventive measures, and Albert B. Smith, a sailmaker, was put shore at La Playa. He reached Presidio Hill undetected, crept up to its summit, and hammered spikes into the touch-holes of the guns.

Encouraged by Smith's success, the men on the *Stonington* rowed ashore, formed in battle array, and moved toward the town. The Mexican defenders retired without offering resistance and occupied Presidio Hill. One of the daughters of the Machado family, who lived in the adobe which still stands on the southwest side of the Plaza, cut the halyards on the flagpole to get the Mexican flag down quickly and save it from disgrace. When the time came to raise the American flag, Smith shinnied up the pole to nail it fast. His action proved symbolic; Old Glory would wave over San Diego henceforth.

In November Commodore Robert Stockton, supreme commander of operations on the coast, arrived in the sixty-gun ship *Congress* to relieve the town of harassment. A Mexican cannon emplaced on the hill dominated the town; their plan was to starve the Americans out by keeping them from roaming in search of food. Santiago Argüello and Miguel de Pedrorena, San Diegans sympathetic to the idea of American domination, led the attack on the Mexican positions and drove their enemy off the hill and up Mission Valley. Stockton strengthened the hilltop earthworks, posted a garrison of a hundred men there, and assigned the site the name of Fort Stockton.

In the meanwhile, the residents of Los Angeles had overthrown their new American masters. While Stockton planned their resubjugation, he received a letter from Warner's Ranch, written by Colonel (later General) Stephen Watts Kearny, who announced his arrival there with the United States Army troops sent overland to con-

Part 4
Yankees
Move In

quer the Far West. A force of 120-odd dragoons, it had been officially designated the Army of the West. On the way to California it had taken New Mexico.

Although Kit Carson (who had ridden East to carry dispatches) was guiding Kearny, Stockton sent a detachment of men to meet the Army of the West, to help bring it in. In the Ballena Valley, the two forces met. On hearing that there was at San Pasqual an encampment of California ranchers who had armed and organized themselves as lancers to oppose the invasion, Kearny decided to come to San Diego via San Pasqual. He intended to take the enemy by surprise there, rather than to approach San Diego unopposed over another route. In the light of his ignorance of the strength of the Californians and the lay of the land, his decision was of questionable wisdom.

Disaster at San Pasqual

As he approached San Pasqual over the hills from the east, Kearny sent scouts ahead to determine the numbers and position of the Californians. The scouts were spotted by a Californian sentry; he gave the alarm to the lancers' commander, Andres Pico. The younger brother of Governor Pio Pico he was, like him, a part time San Diegan.

Kearny, although the advantage of surprise was lost to him, followed through

Gun Carriage.

Limbered for Draft.

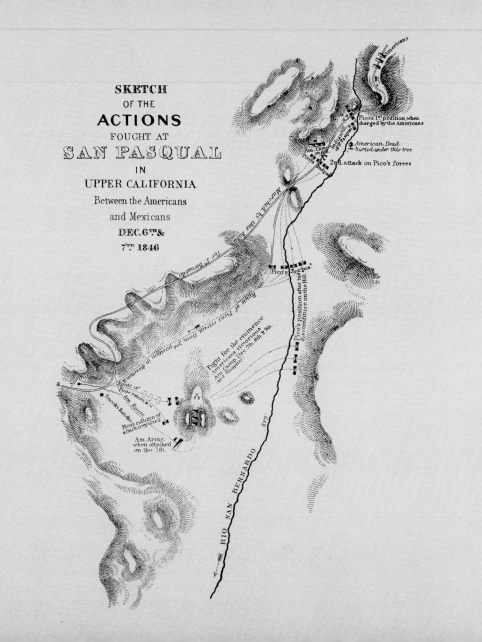

SKETCH
OF THE
ACTIONS
FOUGHT AT
SAN PASQUAL
IN
UPPER CALIFORNIA
Between the Americans
and Mexicans
DEC. 6TH &
7TH 1846

with his plans for an attack. His men, after the long, weary ride across the western deserts, were as haggard as the mules that had carried them. The coastal hills had been as hard on them as the deserts; they had slogged through a chill rain for the last few days. To oppose the lances they had carbines and sabers. The ragged troopers looked anything but warlike as they began their charge down into the valley, while still in column of march. As the Californians were drawn up to meet them a mile and a half away, it was a straggling charge. The Americans' carbines had been wet by the rains, but no orders had been given to draw and replace the charges in them, so when the attempt to discharge them was made, the dragoons found the weapons would not fire; the Army of the West was reduced to short sabers against long lances. Trailing into battle in a column, the Americans were dealt with group by group until enough had been killed to warrant a Californian withdrawal, in order to repeat the pattern; the lancers galloped away, leaving Kearny in possession of a field scattered with his dead. He lost a fifth of his command, Pico lost none, in California's bloodiest battle.

The day after the battle the Army of the West set out for San Diego. Only a few miles along the road the Californians appeared again, driving the Americans to occupy the top of a rocky hill, where they remained surrounded, in desperate plight. With their supplies gone, the soldiers began to kill and eat their tired, faithful mounts; the place has been known ever since as Mule Hill. Kit Carson, Lieutenant Edward Beale of the Navy, and an Indian crept through the Mexican lines to take word of the disaster to Commodore Stockton. Four days after the battle 250 marines and bluejackets arrived at Mule Hill from San Diego, and Pico withdrew.

The Army of the West was escorted into San Diego on December 12. Two weeks and three days later they marched away again, with their rescuers and other naval reinforcements, to retake Los Angeles. After a victory at San Gabriel over a large force that included Pico and his lancers, they entered the City of Angels. General Flores, the leader of the defeated forces, left Andres Pico in command and departed for Sonora. Pico's troops camped on ranches near the pueblo, to prepare for further resistance, but Fremont moved into the San Fernando Valley after a successful campaign in the north. Realizing that his army would be hopelessly crushed by the superior forces, Pico responded to Fremont's invitation to meet at Cahuenga Pass—the scene of many a skirmish in past years—to discuss terms of surrender. On January 23, 1847, Andres Pico capitulated, ending the war in California. The following year, the Treaty of Guadalupe Hidalgo confirmed the United States' hold on the West.

The Mormon Battalion

San Diego was little changed by the conquest. The town remained a Mexican village, holding occasional fiestas and bullfights to break the increasing monotony. The American soldiers' chief influence was on the appearance of the town. Men of the Mormon Battalion, which, after the longest infantry march in history, arrived too late to join in the fighting, whitewashed the town, and built the first brick house in San Diego, on the southwest side of the Plaza. Seventy-eight of the Mormons remained at Fort Stockton when the others were sent to the North, while Company I of Stephenson's New York Volunteers made the old mission their barracks and headquarters. These men conducted the first American census of the county and found there were 248 white residents, 483 converted Indians, 1,550 wild Indians, 3 Negroes, and 3 Sandwich Islanders.

Gold!

Sparked by the Gold Rush, Northern California expanded explosively. Newcomers entered an area where the laws were a confusion of Mexican, American, and improvised codes, administered by officers and courts of the same description, drawing their powers from all manner of odd sources.

There had been no time to replace military rule with territorial government by 1849, and the Gold Rush had brought enough population and problems to require statehood, so General Bennett Riley called together a constitutional convention in August. Miguel de Pedrorena and Henry Hill were chosen to represent San Diego and to have a part in assisting such great figures as John Sutter, Abel Stearns, Mariano Vallejo, Robert Semple, and William Gwin in writing the constitution and setting the boundaries of the state. The constitution was accepted by the people of California in the first election under the American flag, and the state's first governor, Peter H. Burnett, was chosen. Only after considerable political activity and maneuvering in Washington, D.C., which resulted in the Compromise of 1850, was California admitted. President Fillmore signed the bill on September 9, 1850.

San Diego County originally included all of Imperial County, most of Riverside and San Bernardino Counties, and the eastern half of Inyo County. The eastern boundary of California was the eastern boundary of San Diego County to beyond the latitude of Monterey. The area was greater than that of twelve states of the Union. In 1851 the San Bernardino and Inyo sections were cut off because they were too far from the county seat, and the county's area came down to twice that of Massachusetts or New Jersey. Further reductions came in

1893, when Riverside County was created and in 1907, when Imperial County broke away. The county's area has since been slightly less than that of the State of Connecticut. Property in the county was valued at $500,000 in 1850; three quarters of the value was in the little county seat.

The Last Alcalde

In 1850 Joshua Bean, the last *alcalde* under the old system, was elected mayor. When the new city council voted themselves and the mayor $6,800 a year in salaries, Mayor Bean vetoed the measure. A subsequent $2,400 annually for the lot of them he accepted as a more appropriate figure, but even this rate of spending bankrupted the city government in two years. The charter was revoked, and government was vested in a board of trustees.

Another event of the admission year was the recognition by Lieutenant Andrew B. Gray that the best site for a seaport town was on the bay, where the downtown district now lies. The men who joined him in trying to develop the area were Miguel de Pedrorena, José Antonio Aguirre, William C. Ferrell, and William Heath Davis of San Francisco—the famous "Kanaka Davis"— a man of great vision and resources. He was the chief investor in the townsite, which was officially named New Town. For $2,304 the promoters bought 160 acres bordered by the harbor's edge and lines now followed by Front Street and Broad-way. They laid out the streets in that quarter and dedicated the first park in San Diego, now called Pantoja Plaza, at the center of town.

In San Francisco Davis bought a cargo of lumber, bricks, and prefabricated houses that had just arrived from the Atlantic Coast via Cape Horn. He chartered the ship, which was not as yet unloaded, and sent it to San Diego. A wharf and a warehouse were constructed from the lumber, at a cost of $60,000.

Tradition dies hard, and movement to New Town from the settlement below the Presidio failed to develop. Houses became vacant, were torn down or were moved away, and Old Town residents gleefully labelled the tiny new community "Davis' Folly." Old Town, meanwhile, was gaining through the arrival of such solid American merchants as Thomas Whaley and Ephraim W. Morse, who enlivened the scene with their expanding mercantile operations.

Count Haraszthy's Jail

In any up-and-coming western town, a good jail was a necessity. There was an adobe den on the Plaza which would not hold anyone who really wanted to get out of it, so the Common Council opened bids for a stone jail. The low bidders were the Israel brothers, who offered to erect it for $3,000. However, the county's first sheriff, Hungarian Count Agoston Haraszthy, was the son of Councilman Charles Haraszthy, and a

45

bid of $5,000 which he submitted was accepted. The Council explained to the public that the members wanted a good job, not a cheap one. Haraszthy built the jail of cobblestones in mortar containing no cement. Rain so damaged it before completion that the Count appealed for $2,000 more to cover the costs of finishing the building. He got it. One of the first prisoners was the nephew of Mayor Bean, a wild youth named Roy, who later became famous as "the law west of the Pecos." Roy had a jackknife in his pocket. That was all he needed to escape, and to ruin the jail in the process, by cutting a hole in the side of it.

Haraszthy attempted, as sheriff, to collect taxes from San Diego's native population. In November of 1851 Antonio Garra, a chief of the Cupeños (a tribe near the Warner's Ranch area), incited his people to fight to gain their independence. An educated man, he apparently had his own ideas about taxation without representation.

Whites recuperating from various ills at the Hot Springs were tortured and massacred. Other scattered attacks were made, but few tribes showed any interest in cooperating with Garra's stalwarts. Some assisted U.S. Army units and San Diego volunteers in putting down the uprising. On January 10, 1852, Garra was executed by a firing squad at the edge of his grave in the Old Town cemetery.

Journalism—and the Army

In 1851, John Judson Ames brought a printing press to New Town and started publication of the weekly *San Diego Herald,* the town's first newspaper. As New Town slowly died on the vine, he moved his press and his type into quarters fronting on the Plaza in Old Town. There he met, for better or worse, that delightful prankster Lieutenant George Horatio Derby, of the Army's Topographical Engineers.

Derby came here in 1853 to direct construction of a dike to turn the San Diego River from San Diego Bay into False Bay (later re-named Mission Bay) to halt the silting-up of the harbor. It was his writing rather than his engineering, however, which won him a secure place in San Diego's history; already, he was famous as a humorist, writing under the name of "John Phoenix." Ames asked him to take over the *Herald* during its editor's absence on a political visit to San Francisco. Hardly had Ames left when Derby reversed the policy of the staunchly Democratic Ames and carried the county for the Whig ticket. His article and the accompanying illustrations have been printed and reprinted in book form ever since, and placed him in the first rank of American humorous writers.

The decade brought the first hope of a transcontinental railroad reaching the Pacific here. The San Diego & Gila, Southern Pacific & Atlantic Railroad Company was organized by Old Town people to build a road from San Diego to Yuma to meet one of the roads competing for the right to build

John Judson Ames who started publication of the weekly San Diego Herald.

on the southern route.

By Stage and Steamer

As precursors to the railways, the first southern overland mail routes were opened. In 1857 the San Antonio and San Diego line began operations. This was the famous "Jackass Mail," derisively so called by Northern California newspapers because it employed mules to pull vehicles of various descriptions from Texas to the Colorado River, where mail sacks and passengers were packed onto mule-back for the desert and mountain journey to the Old Town Plaza. The great Butterfield stage line from Missouri to San Francisco followed the San Antonio-San Diego route from Texas into San Diego County, where the two lines diverged at Warner's Ranch. Carrizo, Vallecito, and San Felipe were busy stopovers for the mail stages and for immigrant trains until the Civil War broke out. From 1861 to 1865 the southern routes were closed.

After the war John G. Capron of San Diego established stage and mail lines to Los Angeles and Tucson, but sidewheel steamers, which had begun to ply the coastal waters between Panama and San Francisco in Gold Rush days, remained the important link with the outside world. People preferred this more luxurious way to travel, and there was no other way to ship out the grain, fruit, and beef the county produced.

50

Alonzo E. Horton, the man responsible for the re-birth of San Diego's New Town.

San Diego was enough of a port to warrant the establishment of U.S. Lighthouse Number 355, erroneously publicized as "The Old Spanish Lighthouse," on Point Loma in 1855. Below the light, on the beach of Ballast Point, whalers set up a depot to render the oil from the blubber of the California gray whales. The business developed from the time of its inception in the 1850s as a shore station—ships had come to hunt whales before that—until the whalers were forced to move across the channel to North Island, when the government took possession of Point Loma in 1871. After that year the activity declined for two decades into oblivion.

Re-birth of New Town

On April 15, 1867, a shrewd Yankee named Alonzo Erastus Horton stepped off the steamer onto a wharf at New Town. He saw what Gray and Davis had seen, before their time, about where the town should be. Horton was not before his time when he said "The town should be down by the wharf." Because the terms of the Board of Trustees had lapsed and no one could authorize the sale of city lands, and because there was no money to pay for the election, the newcomer put down money to pay the county clerk for the election. Then he bought one thousand acres of what is now downtown San Diego for 27½ cents an acre.

Horton, obviously, was a first-class pro-

The Horton House was a marvel in its day. It cost some $150,000 and had nearly a hundred rooms.

moter. As soon as the townsite was platted he advertised his property widely, gave lots to people whose friendly interest would help his town, erected buildings and a new wharf, and in short order began to sell lots so fast he complained that he grew weary of handling all the money that rolled in; the first real estate boom was under way, and a town faced with false fronts and hitching posts filled bayfront land previously the home of the jackrabbit and horned toad.

San Diego began to think expansively. The trustees set aside 1,400 acres as a city park, and had their act ratified by the State Legislature to frustrate land sharks.

In 1868 the town got another newspaper, the *Herald* having moved with its editor to San Bernardino in 1860. The *San Diego Union's* first issue, that of October 10, 1868, was hailed with rejoicing—by Old Town—for the first publisher cast his fortunes with those of the old adobe county seat. But in 1870 the *Union* moved, as many businesses were doing, to the scene of greater activity, Horton's Addition. In 1871, after much litigation and inter-community feuding, a new county clerk, Chalmers Scott of New Town, quietly moved the county records from the Whaley House in Old Town, which had been the court house and hall of records, to Horton Hall on Sixth Street. That settled the question of which town would be the center of things. The following year a fire destroyed Old Town's largest hotel, the three-story Franklin

House, and other buildings on the south-west side of the Plaza. The little place at the foot of Presidio Hall was left without any hope of competing with the dynamic Yankee town by the bay.

The new county seat by now was well fixed for hotels, of which the leading one was the Horton House, an attractive two-story brick structure which faced a plaza, where the U.S. Grant Hotel now stands. Built by Alonzo Horton, popularly nicknamed "Father" Horton, it cost a fortune—$150,000—and had nearly a hundred rooms.

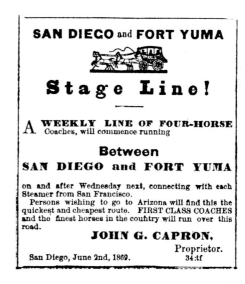

Julian was the center of the San Diego County "Gold Rush" in the 1870s.

"Thar's Gold in Them Hills!"

The discovery of gold in the Julian country during 1870 was a boost to the port and to downtown business. Supplies came in on the steamers, to be freighted up long mountain grades to the mines, and gold went out. For a time it seemed that Julian, founded in 1870, might overshadow San Diego and be the leading community in the county, but there proved to be a limit to the gold in the Cuyamacas.

Then came another boom in 1872, the "Tom Scott Boom," which brought the city's population up to four thousand people. It resulted from a visit to the Horton House by Colonel Thomas Scott, the president of the Texas & Pacific Railroad, which was planning to extend to the Pacific as one of the great transcontinental lines. Scott came to look over possible Pacific termini, and to listen to offers from cities of inducements, in the form of gifts. Enough open land and town property were proffered by the city, the county, and private citizens to elicit a promise to put the Pacific terminus of a great southern system on San Diego Bay. Property values soared. Speculation was rife. However, the expansion of the Texas & Pacific system never came about. The untimely failure of the great railroad speculator Jay Cooke, and the Black Friday panic, discouraged the foreign investors upon whom all such developments depended. The boom burst,

despondency followed, and half of the town's boomtime population left.

In 1879 a group of San Diego and National City businessmen formed a committee to attempt again to bring a transcontinental road into San Diego. Frank Kimball (who with his brother Warren had founded National City) went to Boston to represent the group before the president of the Santa Fe, which then intended to reach the Pacific at Guaymas, Mexico. Kimball sold the Santa Fe road on the idea of coming to Southern California instead, a decision that was never regretted. Perhaps it should be said that he bought them on the idea, for a basic reason for the change of the road's plans was the offer of cash and land made by Kimball to bring the line here.

Coming of the Iron Horse

A subsidy of three million dollars was paid by San Diego and National City people, and seven million dollars worth of property was added to it. This amounted to twice what it cost to build San Diego's first rail connection with the rest of the country, a line called the California Southern. The California Southern ran up the coast to the site of Oceanside, then up Temecula Canyon, toward and through San Bernardino, and over the Cajon Pass to Santa Fe's railhead at Barstow. The road was to be a subsidiary of the Santa Fe. No San Diegan got a share of stock for the contributions made. The only return for the gifts of

Part 5 Boom And Bust

money and land that the railroad made to the two towns was a promise that its main Pacific Coast terminus would always be on San Diego Bay. Kimball actually got a promise that the favored town would be National City. This pledge the then management of the Santa Fe kept only as long as it was convenient. Not long after Santa Fe trains first rolled into Los Angeles—part of the way over California Southern right-of-way, which they still traverse on that run—the City of Angels became the terminus; the shops went to San Bernardino.

The commencement of construction on the California Southern roadbed breathed new life into San Diego. In 1881 the gas company set up its works and began to lay pipes to provide service to all who wanted hot, clean flames for heating and illuminating their homes and offices. In 1882 the telephone company started in business with thirteen subscribers.

September of 1883 saw the completion of the railroad as far as San Bernardino, but winter rains that year ripped out the tracks through Temecula Canyon. Eastern engineers who laid out that stretch had made a mistake often repeated by newcomers to Southern California; they ridiculed local citizens' warnings about how Southern California's washes become real rivers in a good rainy season. Not until November 19, 1885, did San Diego get to celebrate the beginning of through service east. The line only lasted to the next wet

winter, that of 1890-91, when it was washed out again, never to be rebuilt. Tracks were laid from Los Angeles via Santa Ana to Oceanside, and San Diego has since remained the last town on a spur line.

Boom of The Elegant Eighties
It was the coming of California Southern's trains in 1885 which touched off the Great Boom of the Eighties. Buildings spread over the landscape, with "gingerbread" at every turn. San Diego's population rocketed up to 40,000 in 1887. The price of downtown lots doubled and tripled over and over again.

New economic activities which the railroad encouraged in the town and port of San Diego, and the new accessibility of the area from the East, were reasons why strangers poured onto D Street from every incoming train. Another, very important reason was the most equable climate in the United States. San Diegans advertised what William Smythe in his *History of San Diego,* called the one resource which did the most to build the city. That it does not snow here was an attraction to Easterners only rivalled by the fact that it does not rain much, and the sunny summers, winters, springs, and falls are all tempered by pleasant sea breezes.

During a visit here Louis Agassiz, the great naturalist, made a speech at the Horton House in which he said, "This is one of the most favored spots on the earth, and people

will come to you from all quarters to live in your genial and healthful atmosphere."

Modernity raced in with the new residents, merchants, and speculators. Horse car lines commenced operations on D Street in 1886. The first electric cars were put on an Old Town run during the following year. This was truly a pioneer effort; only two towns west of the Mississippi instituted trolley service before San Diego did. Edison's new-fangled incandescent lamps were used to light homes; the streets were illuminated by brilliant arc-lights at the top of 135-foot poles.

On May 3, 1886, by a vote of the people, the city decided to reincorporate. That year there were 340 businessmen and professional firms. In 1887 the number had grown to 987. In 1888 the first modern high dam, the Sweetwater Dam, was built by National

City interests, to begin a new era in providing water for the San Diego area.

One of the greatest benefits of the boom, was that it attracted the interest of John D. Spreckels, a sugar-refining millionaire, to San Diego. In 1886 the Spreckels Brothers Commercial Company opened its warehouse doors on the waterfront. The following year Spreckels bought the Coronado Beach Company, which had begun the development of the transbay community and owned the great Hotel del Coronado.

Dark Days

In the spring of 1888 credit tightened and numbers of land speculators had to offer their holdings for sale, to pay off creditors on whose capital they had been operating. Their need to sell forced prices down, and shattered land values which had been artificially inflated by unrealistic speculation. A great "bust" followed the Great Boom. Ten thousand people left town in the first few months after the bubble broke. Houses stood deserted all over town. Public and private improvement works were suspended, making unemployment a pressing problem.

The upturn soon began, however. The San Diego Flume Company, which had been financed with English capital unaffected by short-term local business cycles, completed their flume from the upper reaches of the San Diego River in 1889. This, with the company's new Cuyamaca

John D. Spreckels and his grandchildren in Coronado. He and his family were intimately associated with San Diego's commercial development.

Dam, was to provide plenty of clear mountain water for the city's expansion. Since the 1870s San Diego had depended on wells downtown, in the canyons of the city park, and most importantly, those of the San Diego Water Company in Mission Valley. Such sources were being exhausted at that time. The flume company's turning to the back country watersheds for city water provided an answer to the ever constant problem that would hold good until the end of World War II. On February 22, 1889, a mammoth celebration was staged over the arrival of Cuyamaca water in the town's system. Fountains 125 feet high rose from nozzles on street corners. Dignitaries commented in their speeches on the crystal clearness and excellent taste of the new water. Some days later the news circulated that air-locks in the mains had prevented the flume water from reaching the town, and the water in the fountains on the day of the celebration had come from the Mission Valley wells just as water had for years. Temporary chagrin on the part of the speechmakers was eclipsed by the joy of the actual arrival of the mountain water.

The electric streetcars of 1887 proved too new and untried to succeed. Two years later a cable car company was incorporated, and soon began to lay tracks from the harbor up Sixth Street, over C to Fourth, and then to University Heights and the Mission Cliff Gardens at the end of Park Boulevard. The company failed in 1892, at a time when Spreckels was buying up the various streetcar companies. He converted horse and cable lines to electric trolleys, rendering the city a great service at a time when it could not have helped itself.

Spreckels' widening investments locally were largely responsible for putting San Diego back into what has become its normal way of life—that of rapid growth. In 1885 he purchased a half-interest in the Otay Water Company. Under the new name of Southern California Mountain Water Company the system supplied San Diego with most of its water, after Spreckels money built a large dam. The system was purchased by the city in 1912.

"The Impossible Railroad"

Spreckels personally took it upon himself to provide San Diego with its yearned-for railroad over the mountains eastward. In 1905 he capitalized the San Diego & Arizona Railroad at six million dollars, and commenced construction. The reluctance of earlier railroad builders (who were motivated by no civic feelings) to come to the Pacific at San Diego, was justified by the fact that it took thirteen years and three times as many million dollars as expected, to build what came to be called "The Impossible Railroad" through Campo and down the spectacularly rugged Carriso Gorge.

In addition to nurturing the growth of San Diego during a difficult period,

Spreckels undertook to advertise and encourage development by buying and publishing the *San Diego Union* and the *Evening Tribune.* He also improved the city's skyline by building, over a number of years, such splendid structures as the Bank of America Building and "the finest theater in the West," the Spreckels.

Other improvements came to San Diego. In 1898 the military reservation on the end of Point Loma, which through the forty-odd years since its establishment had been undeveloped, was fortified against possible enemy attack. The name Rosecrans was assigned to the fort, in honor of a Civil War general who had shown friendly interest in San Diego during the early years of Horton's Addition.

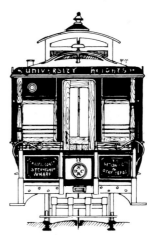

In 1905 occurred one of San Diego's great disasters, the explosion of the boilers of a gunboat, the U.S.S. *Bennington*. Sixty men were killed; they were buried in the Fort Rosecrans National Cemetery, which is still called informally the Bennington Cemetery.

The United States Naval Coaling Station was established on the bay side of Point Loma in 1907. The significance of the new facility was not appreciated then, but the fuel depot was the beginning of the permanent Naval stations here which have been a major support to the economy ever since.

A citrus fruit and truck gardening boom commenced in all earnest during the early years of the twentieth century. Towns like Chula Vista expanded as places where an orchard went with every home. The livestock industry continued to bulk large in the agricultural back country.

World's Fair—and a Flood

The strong will to advertise the city flowered in 1909 into plans to hold an exposition here in 1915, to help celebrate the completion of the Panama Canal. The town's forty thousand inhabitants pushed forward the Panama-California Exposition, against every obstacle, despite the competition of another exposition at San Francisco. It was housed in the most beautiful buildings San Diego had ever seen, ornamented by plaster workers brought over from Italy. The old city park which held the new buildings was extensively landscaped and named for Vasco Nuñez de Balboa, the first white man who crossed the Isthmus of Panama and saw the Pacific.

San Diego got the publicity the fair's backers hoped for. Theodore Roosevelt, William Jennings Bryan, Thomas Edison, and Henry Ford came in 1915. The world's largest municipal structure, Balboa Stadium, got a great deal of mention. The first battleships to enter the harbor put in. Navy men marched in parades and assisted in many ways with the exposition. The result of the fair was that the city became known for its climate and location as an ideal residential community.

In 1916 San Diego's publicity was adverse. The city hired Charles Hatfield, a rainmaker from Glendale, who guaranteed to end a long drought and fill Morena reservoir for $10,000. He set up towers near the lake, and on them he installed mysterious equipment which produced periodic explosions of vapor. In a few days it began to rain. Before it finally stopped, the floods that descended from the heavens washed out Lower Otay Dam, killing a score of people in the valley below and carrying houses to sea on tossing waves. Hundreds were left homeless, in communities isolated by the destruction of most of the county's bridges. San Diego was an island cut off from the world, without road, rail, telephone, and telegraph. Steamers calling at San Diego took away news of the disaster

Part 6
A New
Century

and came back bringing food and emergency supplies. The work of cleaning up and repairing widespread damage and destruction required years. Claiming that the flood was "an act of God," the city refused to pay Hatfield his $10,000.

Camp Kearny, the Navy, and a Zoo

Like the Spanish-American War, World War I brought military construction contracts. Camp Kearny was established on the mesa north of Mission Valley. At Camp Kearny most of the men who went from this area to serve in France were trained. Six million dollars were spent on Fort Rosecrans and North Island, making the port safer from attack. San Diego's desirability as a center for Naval activities was being better appreciated on all levels. In 1919 the Marine Base was dedicated. In 1921 the Naval Training Station came into being on

land given to the Government by the city and Chamber of Commerce. The Eleventh Naval District was created in 1922, with San Diego as its headquarters.

Another development was taking shape. A menagerie of animals left by the 1915 exposition was the core of the new San Diego Zoo, which Dr. Harry Wegeforth was coaxing into existence. No one imagined then that city cooperation in the form of a tax to support the Zoo, as well as private contributions and patronage, would build it into the largest in the world.

The Aircraft Industry

Few paid much attention on May 10, 1927, when a young airmail pilot took off from St. Louis in a monoplane which the Ryan Aeronautical Company of San Diego had built for him. Eleven days later, although he was now six thousand miles away, San Diego — and the whole world — made a great fuss over him. Charles A. Lindbergh had landed in Paris after the first solo transatlantic flight in history, and San Diego was on the aviation map in a big way.

October 25, 1935, was an even greater day in local air history. On that day Consolidated Aircraft Corporation—now Convair— moved here from Buffalo, N.Y., and dedicated its new plant. It soon became the city's largest civilian employer. Its growth, together with that of Ryan, Solar, and Rohr Aircraft, has been a vital influence in the city's life.

KEEP OUT
OF THE WATER

He did!
OFFICIAL PHOTO
BY ERICKSON.

Charles A. Lindbergh.

Charles A. Lindbergh following his historic flight. Right, President Franklin D. Roosevelt attends San Diego's 1935 Exposition with Mrs. Roosevelt.

A Second Fair

What occupied the interest of every San Diegan in 1935, however, was the California Pacific International Exposition. Twenty years after San Diego's first World's Fair the second one opened to a crowd of 60,000; the date was May 28. Theodore Roosevelt had visited the 1915 fair, and President Franklin D. Roosevelt visited the second, to address a capacity crowd in Balboa Park stadium. The fair was a tremendous success and served to advertise San Diego's charms to another generation.

The depression slowed the city's growth, which had been based largely upon people who were in a position to move into an area of their own choosing. The decade following 1929 was one whose economic conditions permitted far less of such growth. Census figures for 1930 and 1940 reflected the first ten-year period in the twentieth century in which the population had not doubled.

NRA
MEMBER
U.S.
WE DO OUR PART

Part 7 Modern Times

The second World War stepped up gains tremendously. The local aircraft plants attracted workers from all over the country. Consolidated became one of the largest airframe factories in the world. Army, Navy, and Marine activities brought tremendous installations and great concentrations of men within the city limits. Camp Callan stretched five miles along the Torrey Pines Mesa, to house Army artillerymen during their training. Camp Elliott was set up on Camp Kearny Mesa to train Marines. The Marine Base and Naval Training Center were enlarged enormously. A new Marine reservation, Camp Pendleton, north of Oceanside, was the world's largest. Houses, streets, and theaters were crowded with military and civilian newcomers to California.

While some wondered about what would happen to San Diego when peace came, far-sighted citizens already were planning for that day, Down through the years, from mission times through those of Davis' Folly and the days of the flume, to the atomic age, such plans always have hinged upon a supply of water. By the 1940s, the rain which fell on San Diego County was being used up by the population, so far as it was practicable to collect it in reservoirs and dams.

It was fortunate that, during the Coolidge administration, Congressman Phil Swing of San Diego foresaw the requirements of the future, and co-authored the bill to provide funds for the construction of Hoover Dam, on the Colorado River. Twenty years later, when the water was sorely needed, it was only 71 miles away, where the aqueduct to Los Angeles passes through San Jacinto, in Riverside County. The first barrel of a two-pipe line to San Diego was completed in 1947, and almost immediately was taxed to capacity. In 1954 the second barrel was finished; three years later both barrels were overloaded, and the need for water still grew. By 1959 San Diego was drawing more than its allotted share from the Colorado, and fear grew that Los Angeles would need its own full quota before San Diego could develop other sources. Hopes then were entertained that water could be drawn from the rainy mountains of Central and Northern California. San Diegans led in a statewide fight to bring in water from the north, against strong opposition in the state

The end of the war, with its prospects of advanced technologies, was a great break with the past. San Diego assimilated its wartime growth as a permanent, not temporary accretion, and became a truly different place. The leading citizen of the old San Diego, George W. Marston, died in 1946, a sadly symbolic loss. He had come during the earliest years of Horton's Addi-tions, had founded the Marston Company and been one of the finest representatives of the business community for over three quarters of a century. Among his many con-

V.J. Day in San Diego, 1945.

tributions to San Diego were Presidio Park and the Junípero Serra Museum.

Post-war development included the disappearance of the streetcars in 1949 and their replacement by buses. Condemned for adding to the congestion of downtown streets, and for costing too much in right-of-way upkeep, the streetcars' disappearance was greeted with as much pride as their debut. Yet many San Diegans regretted the passing of the fast, whirring trolleys, which gave rapid, comfortable service, especially on interurban runs.

Tuna Down, Port Tonnage Up

In the 1950s the fishing fleets diminished, after contributing a great deal to the community's economic life. The successful fishermen of early New Town had been the Chinese, who built junks here for local use. Forbidden to own boats by anti-Asiatic laws, they were supplanted by the Portuguese and Italians. In 1911 a growing market for tuna forced prices up to $100 a ton on a previously little-eaten product. A cannery was opened, and fishermen thought of nothing else but tuna. After years of steady increases in the industry, 1950 saw 200 boats (worth up to half a million dollars each) supply six local canneries with $30,000,000 worth of tuna, making San Diego the leading fishing port in the United States. Such success invited competition. Japanese and South Americans, benefiting from low wage

Tuna boats in port, 1950s. Overleaf, San Diego in the 1960s.

scales and less demanding employees, cut so heavily into San Diego's markets that, by 1960, only one cannery was left in operation and it was occupied with putting up imported frozen tuna.

In other respects maritime activities increased, particularly in the handling of exports of Imperial Valley and Mexican cotton. Broadway and B Street Piers, the existing municipal terminals, were augmented when a nine-and-a-half million dollar bond issue was passed in 1955; it financed a 96-acre terminal at the foot of Tenth Avenue. Port tonnage figures rose, and cargoes diversified. Bunkering facilities, on other than a limited basis, were provided for the first time.

The late 1950s also saw the beginning of a major shipbuilding industry when the National Steel & Shipbuilding Corporation, previously engaged in building small vessels, won government contracts for the construction of C-3 type freighters with passenger accommodations. First of these vessels, the 10,000-ton *Export Agent,* slid down the ways on January 30, 1960.

The aircraft industry remained a mainstay of the local economy, although the late 1950's saw the beginning of a trend toward the production of unmanned missiles as defensive and offensive weapons.

Scientists and Tourists

Consolidated Aircraft, after various mergers, became a subsidiary of General

Dynamics. Another subsidiary, General Atomic, opened the John Day Hopkins Laboratory for Pure and Applied Science. The U.S. Naval Electronics Laboratory on Point Loma was the largest single Navy activity devoted to electronic research and development. The Scripps Institution of Oceanography at La Jolla became internationally known for research in its field. San Diego became, during the 1950's, a center for research into ways to create a fuller life for humanity in the future.

Still a tourist center and a developing one, San Diego drew almost $150,000,000 annually from tourism. Nevertheless, of the income of San Diego as a community, seventy-eight percent was derived directly or indirectly from defense expenditures by the Federal Government. International disarmament proposals, and defense economy measures, caused San Diegans to ponder upon what should be the direction of future economic growth.

However, during the third quarter of the twentieth century, the world did not disarm. By 1984 one out of every five dollars of the gross regional product (the total of goods and services produced in the area) came from the Pentagon. The total for that year was $6.5 billion, of which $3.26 billion was in the form of defense department contracts, $1.66 billion was active duty payroll, and $662 million was civilian payroll. All of that money turned over in the local economy many times, so San Diego remained as economically dependent on the military as it had been in times past.

Manufacturing, if production for the military is figured in, was the leading producer of income locally during the third quarter of the twentieth century, as it had been during the second. The total dollar value of San Diego's manufactured products was $8 billion for the year of 1984. Non-military industrial sales came to $4.74 billion. Most of that was in the form of high tech products and instrumentation.

San Diego had become a center for such sophisticated production partly as a result of the development of increasingly distinguished faculties and splendid research facilities at local institutions of higher education.

The San Diego campus of the University of California actually started during those years. It was in 1964 that the University of California at San Diego accepted its first undergraduate students. (It grew from the Scripps Institution of Oceanography, a branch of the University since 1912.) The school of medicine, the third in the university system, opened in 1968.

By 1984 UCSD was one of the top research institutions in the country. It is sixth in the nation among all colleges and universities in the amount of federal funds allocated for research. There are five Nobel prize laureates associated with the campus and 46 members of the National Academy of Sciences.

The San Diego-Coronado Bay Bridge opened in 1969.

San Diego State University, which began as a normal school in 1897 grew to be one of the largest institutions of higher learning in the state, with an enrollment of 33,000 in 1985. By then it accounted for 25 percent of the funded research in the California state university system. It was the first school in the system to offer a doctor's degree and is nationally recognized as one of the best schools of business administration.

After manufacturing and military and governmental activities, the third industry, in terms of dollars earned had become by the 1980s, tourism. The beaches and the world famous zoo continued to attract people as they had in the past and the development of Sea World in Mission Bay Park and the establishment of Old San Diego State Park added to the appeal of San Diego to people from places with less agreeable climates. Most visitors came from other parts of Southern California and from Mex-ico. In 1984 almost 29 million visitors spent over $2 billion here.

With the completion of a convention center on the bay projected for 1988, tourism is expected to loom larger in the economic life of the southwest corner of the United States in years to come. That is viewed by old and new residents with mixed feelings, since many who come as tourists are likely to want to stay, and growth has brought its problems.

The Future

The controlling factor in San Diego's history during this century has been growth. In 1900 the population of the county was 15,000. By 1980 it was 1,861,800. The projected population at the end of the century is 2,699,300, which is almost 1,800 times more than in 1900. And that growth is expected to continue into the indefinite future at the same rate.

Demographers predict that the nature of the area's population will change. People over 65 years of age will make up a larger proportion of the general population, 12.8 percent by the year 2000, as opposed to 10.3 percent in 1980.

Minorities—mostly Asian and Hispanic—will account for 60 percent of the population growth between 1985 and the year 2000, when whites will make up a slim majority of 51 percent.

Among the disadvantages the growth in

population will bring with it is increased air pollution. By 1990 the steps being taken to deal with the problem will be outweighed by the increase in motor vehicles, and the air quality will start to deteriorate then, if present trends continue.

Other unpleasantness is anticipated. Richard Huff, executive director of the San Diego Association of Governments has said, "Probably the most visible image of our future will be rush-hour traffic jams of exasperating proportions on interstate highways and surface streets throughout the region."

In 1985 nine miles of freeways were burdened with bumper-to-bumper traffic at rush hours. In twenty years that daily traffic jam is expected to extend over 100 miles, centering on downtown and Mission Valley.

It appears clear now that the San Diego area, which has become dependent on the automobile for personal transportation, will have to turn to other modes to provide its citizens mobility in the future. For that reason the electric railway returned to San Diego. The San Diego and Arizona right-of-way was acquired by the San Diego Metropolitan Transit Development Board and interurban passenger service on it between downtown and the Mexican border commenced in 1981. The operation has been successful and popular. As a result, expansions of the system along the major traffic corridors in the county are planned to help deal with the problem of transporting the three million people expected to live in the area early in the twenty-first century.

The increased use of public transportation, including the bus systems, holds promise as a partial solution also of the impending traffic and air pollution problems. Another partial solution lies in having people live closer to their work. Advances are being initiated in that regard, with major housing projects now going into the redeveloping downtown area.

In the past San Diego has grown and prospered because its superb climate and situation on the shore of the Pacific have made it one of the pleasantest places to live in North America. The next few decades are clearly going to be pivotal in the history of our city. The beauty that has blessed past generations of San Diegans is in the hands of the present generations, through their elected representatives, to preserve or to destroy. At the present time their decision has not been clearly and finally made.

The author of this book, James R. Mills, was, at the time he wrote it, the curator of the San Diego Historical Society's Junípero Serra Museum, a position he held from 1955 to 1960, when he left the employ of the Historical Society to run for the state assembly in the 79th district. He was elected and served until 1966, when he ran for the state senate, where he represented San Diego County until 1982.

During his 22 years as a member of the California legislature he left his own mark on the history of San Diego. He was the author of the legislation that created the Old San Diego State Park and the San Diego light rail system (the San Diego trolley). He was responsible for the state appropriation of $500,000 for the restoration of the Old Globe Theater after it was destroyed by fire in 1978, and that state appropriation triggered a federal contribution, without which the project could not have been undertaken. He was also responsible for appropriations that built the library building at San Diego State University and the Third College campus at the University of California at San Diego, which he helped legislatively to establish.

While a member of the legislature he served as chairman of the majority caucus in both houses of the legislature and as chairman of the rules committee in both houses. He also acted as the elected chief of the senate for ten years, being president pro tempore from January of 1971 to December of 1980.

San Diego: Where California Began was first published as Volume V, Number 1 (the January 1959 issue) of the *San Diego Historical Society Quarterly.* It has since then passed through four editions. This new one has been extended by Senator Mills to cover the years between 1959 and 1985.

James R. Mills

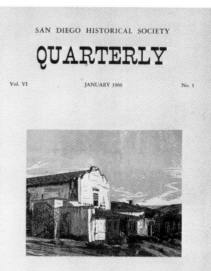

SAN DIEGO HISTORICAL SOCIETY

QUARTERLY

Vol. VI   JANUARY 1960   No. 1

SPECIAL EDITION

SAN DIEGO . . .
WHERE CALIFORNIA BEGAN